GODS OF DISHARMONY

R. Nikolas Macioci

For Sandra Ditschle who encouraged me to turn these poems into a book. Thank you

Acknowledgements

Blue Unicorn—Anton Webern (1883-1945)

Contents

GODS OF DISHARMONY

I like to read about composers' lives,
who they were, how they lived and died.
Learning about them helps me define myself.
I Googled, and there they were, composers
with the most bizarre conduct. I expected
peculiar comportment but nothing
as unusual as what I read.

Satie owned over a hundred umbrellas,
eighty-four handkerchiefs, and would eat
only white foods. Richard Wagner was
a cross dresser who surrounded himself
with rose-scented, pink cushions. Philip
Heseltine smoked dope, wrote satiric
limericks about other composers, and
committed suicide at age thirty-six.
Frantise Kotzwara engaged the services
of a prostitute and asked her to cut off
his penis. When she refused, he asked
her to hang him from a rope to increase
his passion while they had sex. She was
charged with murder but acquitted. Mozart
had Tourette's Syndrone marked by a
condition known as Coprolalia, the
uncontrollable and obsessive use of
obscene language. Often he would
meow like a cat. Mahler was considered
a genius at picking fights. Beethoven

was notoriously messy, and the smell
from his apartment wasn't too nice either.

Do these stories lead me to accept
idiosyncrasies of genius, or do they lead
to disappointment of human frailty?
Did I make a mistake looking behind
Gods of Disharmony

the curtain of these lives? Sometimes, truth
can be an enthralling ugliness that speaks
beyond time's historic facade. These men
created beauty from warped hearts and
malformed selves, and their strangeness
may well have been the impetus for producing
<u>incomparable Art.</u>

PETER ILYICH TCHAIKOVSKY
(1840-1893)

He suffered emotional trauma that
lasted his whole life because he had been
separated from his mother when in
The School of Jurisprudence. Then. he sat
for days and cried when she died. He was, at
most, fourteen, and he became very thin.
Owing to grief, the pallor of his skin
gave him an unhealthy appearance. Flat
out lies about his death persist, but pale
against new found evidence that he took
his own life by drinking poison before
old classmates who feared that he would unveil
his liaison or give another look
to a nephew of Duke Stenback-Thurmor.

CLAUDE VIVIER (1947-1983)

He writes incantatory notes on the
page, much of it learned from Stockhausen in
Cologne. His inspired harmonies begin
to shimmer in a way that sets him free
to invent language, orchestrations, be
prophetic about a knife against skin.
That music's motif will then underpin
his plot of money, sex, and thievery.
He closes the piano on *Do you*
Believe in the Immortality of
the Soul and steps into the street. Lean men
lounge against the bar in a room of blue
smoke. Pascal Dolzan promises him rough love,
stabs him again and again and again.

HUGO WOLF (1860-1903)

His syphilis has turned into a dark
abyss. The failure of iodine and
mercury limits the amount of sand
in his life's hourglass, most surely will mark
the end of his composing. Brown as bark
on a tree, the river awaits his planned
suicide, but a stranger lends a hand
and stumble-walks him to a nearby park
before he can commit the act. The pain
of ulcers occurs, causing confusion
in his mind. He can't read and he can't sleep.
It's as if rabid rats stir in his brain.
In the asylum, slow death has begun.
He hears through the walls the insane who weep.

HENRY PURCELL (1659-1695)

It's been a difficult rehearsal. At
last, lights dim on *Dido and Aeneas*,
but Henry is inclined to dalliance
as well as a round or two of chitchat.
By midnight, he dons his opera hat
and wool muffler. It is with happiness
that he leaves the theater ambiance
and starts towards his Marsham Street habitat.
Outside, it is past zero cold, and snow
obscures the moon like white acrobats. He
braves the blizzard with undaunted will.
Head down against the gales, he does not know
that his wife has locked him out with no key
and that within weeks he will die from chill.

KAREL KOMZAK II (1850-1905)

Born in Prague, his long-standing desire to
inhabit Vienna is fulfilled in
1882, a time when he's been
named bandmaster. His fame is indeed due
to his friendly nature and his breakthrough
conducting, energetic and akin
to lively and dynamic. Fame again
grows more and more, making him the kingpin
of military composers, and the
climax of his career: a series of
concerts in Missouri. There he reveals
his grave fatigue. Six months later, when he
tries to jump on a departing train, shove
<u>forward, he slips and falls under the wheels.</u>

JOHN BARNES CHANCE (1932-1972)

Serving in Seoul, South Korea as a
U.S. Army Band arranger, he came
across a Korean folk song, the same
one that would serve as inspiration, play
a big part in his best known work. Away
from the army, his self-evident fame
gave him the opportunity to claim
a position in Greensboro. The day
his success ended was by accident.
In his backyard he was putting up the
poles for a tent. Sweat running down his chest,
one metal pole slipped out of control, went
against an electrified fence, and he
<u>died instantly of cardiac arrest.</u>

ERNEST CHAUSSON (1855-1899)

His wealthy family approved of his law
career, but, at twenty-five, he turned to
music and therein discovered his true
vocation. Many years passed and the claw
of creativity began to paw
his brain like an insistent cat to do
an orchestral piece, and so he drew
on works of Wagner, Brahms, Franck and his raw
inspiration to compose the *Poeme for
Violin and Orchestra.* One spring day,
he was taking a break from writing the
Celeste, mounted his bicycle and tore
down an uncommonly steep byway.
<u>He hit a brick wall and died instantly.</u>

LOUIS VIERENE (1870-1937)

Born with congenital cataracts, he
was nearly blind. At age two he played a
lullaby on the piano. He may
have been unlucky with his vast degree
of physical difficulty, but the
position of organist would someday
be his at Notre-Dame, and he does stay
there until 1937. Three
hours into his concert, he pitched forward
on June 2nd, fell off the bench. His footing
hit the low "E" petal. A steady stream
of sound throughout the cathedral was heard
a while. He died at the organ, putting
<u>in effect his oft-stated life long dream.</u>

JEAN-BAPTISTE LULLY (1632-1687)

He is the favorite of the Sun King,
Louis XIV's court composer. Tonight,
a well powdered and wigged Lully, in spite
of rumors and after their suppering,
slips into the king's own chambers. That wing
of the palace knows the king's habits, right
or wrong, and keeps eyesight downward. Pure white
curtains surround the illicit bed. Spring
shimmers with a rainbow array amid
flower gardens of Versailles, but Louis
is ill and unaffected by the scene.
Weeks pass, The king recovers and has bid
him to conduct. With sharp pointed staff he
stabs his own right foot and dies of gangren.

WALLINGFORD RIEGGER (1885-1961)

It is 1957, and he
is being investigated by an
anti-communist committee. The man
behind it is Joseph McCarthy. The
committee exculpates Riegger. Though free
to return to his musical world, can
he ever regain control of more than
a very small amount of dignity?
Leonard Bernstein honors him, conducting
his Music for Orchestra with the New
York Philharmonic Orchestra. Riegger
walks to the theater because it's spring,
trips over the tangled leashes of two
dogs, hits his head and does not recover.

ANTON WEBERN (1883-1945)

Disillusioned with Hitler's tight control,
Anton and his family have fled from
Vienna to Mittersill. They have come
on this particular night to extol
their daughter's cuisine. After dinner, whole
stories are told about how minds are numb
from brainwashing without a single crumb
of truth and that truth was never the goal.
A sudden knock at the door brings old fear,
but it's two American soldiers who
want to speak with the son-in-law who's led
outside. The fall night is chilly but clear.
Anton steps out for a cigar, curfew
ignored. The soldier sees light, shoots him dead.

GUILLAUME LEKEU (1870-1894)

In his own words he said that joy is a
lot harder to paint than suffering. He,
in his very short life, had only three
major influences that led the way
to his melancholy tendency. They
were Beethoven, Wagner, and Franck. Though free
to experiment, he never did see
enough years to study music and stray
beyond the norm. Sorbet killed him one night
after his 24th birthday. Tainted
sorbet led to typhoid fever. Guillaume
had headaches, stomach pain, and tried to fight
the fever which was so high he fainted
and died in his bed in his parents' home.

GIOVANNI BATTISTA PERGOLESI
(1710-1736)

His comic opera, when performed in
Paris, prompted the dire "quarrel of the
comic actors" between those who agree
with comic opera and the then thin
margin of people who had always been
exposed to serious opera. Be
that as it may, the definite degree
of his fame let comic opera win.
His young life was cut extremely short by
tuberculosis. Then, there was no cure,
and many died from the disease. No tricks
of medicine reduced his fever. Sky
turned black with his death. Though he will endure,
when he died he was only twenty-six.

ENRIQUE GRANADOS (1867-1916)

He is invited to the White House by
President Woodrow Wilson to give a
piano recital. He first will play
his own fandango. He straightens his tie
and begins. His lean, limber fingers fly
over the keys like startled birds. Halfway
through, there is an intermission. Gourmet
food is served before they say farewell. Try
as they may, he and his wife miss the ship,
board the Sussex ferry to England, on
from there to France, and then back to Spain. Sound
of alarms blare. A German sub does rip
out the side of the Sussex, and at dawn
with a life-long fear of oceans, he drowned.

ALEXANDER BORODIN (1833-1887)

He was born in Saint Petersburg as an
illegitimate son of a sixty-
two-year-old, Georgian nobleman. He
married a twenty-five-year-old woman.
The nobleman had an extensive plan
to register Alexander with the
serf, Porfiry Borodin. He was free
of serfdom at seven, but his lifespan
was cut short by poor health. He had had three
minor heart attacks and cholera. Chill
brought on more ill health, but in the late fall,
with the help of medicine, he did see
his way clear to dance his last dance until
he fell dead at the academy ball.

MAURICE RAVEL (1875-1937)

His last work will end in a crescendo.
In his own words, it will consist wholly
of "orchestral tissue" and will be
"without music." It will start somewhat slow,
be consistent throughout, and likely go
on for seventeen minutes, being free
of convention. Picking up his pen, he
writes at the top of the page "Bolero."
It's October 8th, 1932.
He's in a cab traveling in Paris. Thrown
against the window when one more cab flies
into the side of his, he gets a few
stitches, but later, a tumor has grown.
From the severe head injury, he dies.

ALEXANDER SCRIABIN (1871-1815)

He made his last public appearance in
St. Petersburg on April 2, the
year he died. Just a few days later, he
noticed a pimple the size of a pin
on his upper lip. Though he had not been
to a doctor, he assumed he was free
of infection, but five days later, three
doctors pronounced it infected. His thin
lip swelled, and he was bed ridden. Heart rate
increased; fever raged; blood poisoning had
set in. Soon after, he died. Even though
he had the best care, the poison went straight
to his brain. What was explicitly sad?
Unfinished work lay on the piano.

CHARLES VALENTIN ALKIN (1813-1888)

A child prodigy, he entered the famed
Conservatoire de Paris before he
was six. He was the first to include the
folk melodies of Jewish music aimed
at creating Art Music. He reclaimed
the Bible, translating the whole book, free
of flaws, into French, now lost like the three
dozen musical compositions. Named
the most eminent representative
of modern piano, with weary blood
he went into seclusion at a grim
period of his life, needing to live
stressless. He died reaching for the Talmud
when a bookcase toppled over on him.